Dusted Words

Dusted Words

ALISA HUTTON

978-0-9953034-0-9 (sc)
978-0-9953034-1-6 (e)

Publisher Name: Alisa Hutton
Publisher Address: 3253 East 28th Avenue,
Vancouver, British Columbia, Canada, V5R 1T1
Publisher Phone Number: 604 367 7427
Legal Name: Alisa Hutton

Lulu Publishing Services rev. date: 12/20/2016

Contents

"The women whom I love and admire for their strength and grace did not get that way because shit worked out. They got that way because shit went wrong, and they handled it. They handled it in a thousand different ways on a thousand different days, but they handled it. Those women are my superheroes."

-Elizabeth Gilbert

The Protagonist

In sudden wave

Rolling over in comfortable tale

Sadness and fear

Breathe deep, close your eyes

Float with storm

No need to slay

No invitation for slaughter

Expand and contract with equal assurance

Trust buoyancy with as much love

As you trust muted bottom

You are the protagonist

She, who is you

Writes this story

Just Breathe

Just breathe

Darkness comes every day

I promise tomorrow there will be light

Just rest

When you feel like you are dipping under waves

Your tired limbs full of lead

Exhale your fight

Close your eyes, just float

The sadness that won't lift

Leave it

Let the tears win today

We will use them to wash our mirrors of clarity

Wringing our hands of sadness

When all feels like it is falling apart

Let it

You have a friend who won't let you sink

Darkness comes every day

We will breathe

Together

My Son

I lazily went to bed one night with a brazen comfort of life

Confidently closing my eyes to sleep, this world I surely did know

Only to be awakened the next morning by a tiny little soul

Mirroring my once younger brown eyes,
someone with a familiar pull

My heart filling effortlessly forgetting all I once did know

Here we were

Who was to teach?

Who was to learn?

A parent's confused role

With just one tick and a following tock

Humbled by your soul, a vulnerable being

I learned to live, I learned to love

All confines of fear, quickly fleeing

My 3 AM giggles and sunrise rendezvous,'
arms wrapping me with purity

Kind soulful eyes bursting with so much
life, words not required to speak

An explosive joy tingling the darkest days back to life

Washing me over, grateful with love to be alive

You; my deepest breath, my precious gift

I sit here today, looking in those same brown eyes

I faintly remember a long time ago

An almost surreal fictional story of a life I used to know

As I squint into past, my love for you
quickly fills up my once emptiness

Hard to imagine this old heart of mine could fill any more

There is not a moment that goes by that my heart doesn't know

My beautiful son

I have been given the gift of every star in the sky

To call myself Mother, to call you my Son,
does not capture either role

All I have learned about love and life came
from your tiny beautiful soul

She Was the Girl

She was the girl

You didn't need to check in on

Her smile seemingly repellent to emotional assault

Always enough to lift you both

Sip from my spirit until you see it in your own eyes again

Take extra she would say, I'll do just fine with less

Arms extended and open in kind, don't
worry I have enough to share

A heart bursting with life reaching past and
beyond attempts at ill intention

Fill yourself up, you will need it to thrive

My love is big, I can live with little

A day no different than any other

A cup of her morning coffee, make it two

Always black, severed with quiet thoughts

Hold the sugar

Her smile today didn't come

Spirit seemed to drift away in your dreams

A heart, now only part

She isn't sure who borrowed it all

She was the girl

You didn't need to check in on

The Tick

Intention to devour imbedded in burrows of
effortless, uniformed kind words

Acceptance neatly tied is gloss wrap

Purchasing the right to politely ravage worth, due to difference

Pretty florals left on a door step in good thought

I can now tell you how wonderful you
are at your needed convenience

My head resting on your lap in ask of nurture

Quietly keep score for the next time you
need on-demand attention

Furiously throwing my disregarded self
against the freshly painted white walls

Pick a team and learn to play the game or lose

Jump

How high

Don't ask questions

Like a good intentioned Buddhist monk walking in the forest

A small tick embeds itself quietly, nesting to feast

Lyme disease left for praise at the altar of compassion

Blood is blood

The Buddhist doesn't kill the tick by nature

Yet the tick freely bequeaths disease with no regard to kindness

Fear

Ego

Jump

How high

Shh, I said don't ask questions

She Already Has

Drenched in an enchanted love

Longing for her familiarity

A past life agreement, let's meet again

Try

Eyes recognized by quiet expression of souls

A gentle tap on the shoulder of subconscious

Without any announcement of her devotional appearance

Hush

Be quiet the universe will only whisper once

A tender feeling, a knowing glance,
recognizable laughter, a familiar smile

She will feel like home; warm, safe, right

Sliding doors, speak to her in your dreams

She will feel you

Send her love letters in a bottle; toss them
without caution in to her sea

She will hear you

You agreed to meet again, if you are quiet, she will find you

She already has, many times before

Shards

The day my glass castle shattered

I placed you in a marble jar containing swept up shards

You do remember that night in May

I was so fragile and you without care

Dressed in my trust, swinging your rusted hammer

I laid wide-eyed and lifeless in blank stare

Wondering in a daze where my head and heart had landed

Something you didn't see as you walked away

The eyes on the back of your head choosing to stay closed

Just me and my soul to remember that day

Lacking the spine required to turn and observe with any love

I sealed the lid of your common jar
with instruction to be read slowly

Danger

Do

Not

Open

Better to be reminded

Every so often I peer in to the dark where
you had carefully been placed

Memories collecting thin layers of dust settling in my own time

My hope

One day the dirty particulates would
cover the view of you and me

Squinting in wish, the memories inside
will one day no longer be my own

A Sunday in spring you decided your collecting
dust was heavy in guilty weight

You climbed out, sitting comfortably in my new space

Shaking your dust on my now clean walls
tempting me with your fate

Ignoring the label I had written on the
jar, I slipped my hand inside

Shards of glass slicing me open easily one more time

Isn't it curious that sometimes bleeding
is the thing we need to feel?

To remind us of the people who cut so very deeply

Where love is never real

Hustle

Planted in seed when my eyes were big and hands small

Attention, hustle

Nurture, hustle

Love, hustle

My eyes lack their once luster

My hands grew larger and worn with callous

My smile merely a flash for someone else's photo album

One day I simply got tired

Attention, nurture, love

Packed neatly in a bag of half-empty memories

My childlike pangs of hope

Left at the curb

With my hustle

Wax Figure

Stale air surrounds him, his skies sheathed in grey

He kisses you with an uncomfortable dampness

Lacking in love, sincerity left at childhood's door

Gracing you with his cold weight, his burden is yours to carry

Dead flowers left on your doorstep, be sure to give your thanks

Inviting empathetic muses in for undignified
assaults, calling it sport

Kind souls always the favored flavor on
his sharp teeth and glass palate

Filling you with wet promise and wringing
you out in pathological flex

A dark tailor who slowly stitches you closed

Your eyes with vengeful pointed silver needles

Your mouth with controlled black thread

Each poke and stich leaving the tiniest drops of your blood

Dear woman, enjoy the taste as your spirit drips

Your heart his final masterpiece

As easy as snuffing a candle, your light now gone

Once the flicker ceases to beat

Once the submission of his muse and stitching complete

Once they sit in wax form lacking any visible soul

In his leathered skin smoking his cancerous
stick, taking one final drag

He wonders why the perfect wax figure he once called wife

Left him all alone to sit in his darkness
for the rest of his heinous life

Southern Comfort

She arrives across border unexpectedly
with the evening summer breeze

I feel that familiar slow southern stare as she walks in the door

Many years between the evenings she
last painted me with her colors

It was our kept secret, an arrangement of mutual affection

Slowly brewed on sangria and slow, subtle dance

I, to adore her nature and only speak of it in written form

That unmatched feminine magnetic pull, eyes collapsing
you and all sensibilities effortlessly to your knees

She, like a gentle purring cat waiting to pounce on its prey

She delights in watching my usual cool nature
twist and spin in nervous foolishness

With a wink of her knowing melt she softly
states, so good to see you again

The room of on-lookers curious of our thick
connection, with few words spoken

I know my place in this game we have played before

Lie on your back and let her rub your belly

Like the sun you don't question her warmth, you
simply close your eyes and appreciate it

The only communication she is interested in, yes ma'am

She will politely ask you to follow, don't
kid yourself you have no choice

Lean in, it is her unmistakable charm

Her passion and grace untethered by a
potion of gratitude and trust

You never know when you will see her
again, don't ask and don't wait

She will arrive when the stars tell her to

Her intuition of you, clock work

The woman who taught me to feel in verse

Never ceased to remind me

I am incredibly alive

My Southern comfort

Stand Alone

You do not know the loss she feels

Your heart's goals to simply suffocate until hope exhales

Psychology and intuition met, speaking when you were not able

Welcome love, sit on my lap

Let me read to you your hellish fable

Loyalty and ownership purchased with abusive
currency, I think you called it trust?

Your mouth and mind sipping on your bitter past

Dressed with a scowl, a must

Drinking down your darkened future

Fermentation that went inexplicably wrong

Igniting your hollow empty shell, lit with
boundless anger and spite

Relishing in your spills of blood, ravaging
faith with your pointless fight

Spitting out crushed souls like yesterday's
fattening, regurgitated lunch

She thought her sacrifice would quench your
thirst, her sadness not quite enough

Go at her one more time, just because, one last emotional punch

Of course you could not

Of course you would not

Leave the children alone

Your beast called trauma, nibbling on their tiny little bones

As she did when she said goodbye, those
little people will eventually grow

They will stand taller than you with eyes wide
open, her love still warm with glow

She will remind them of the gifts they share and
the connections that will always bind

So stand alone in your dark, wrapped
comfortably in your violence

Shh, be quiet, all aboard, the next stop your total silence

Wait for it, they will come, the unashamed voices

Don't forget life's reminder

We all make our choices

You once knew hearts of goodness, genuine
laughter and spirts made of kind

Breathe it in and breathe it deep, for one day you will find

The only thing you have left to live with

Is that darkness in your mind

Silence

4am welcomed, gasping for air

Wake up now, I care not for your needed rest

Dear human, extreme sadness does not sleep

In silence you feel the crack and rip of your
chest, expanding in all the wrong ways

An invisible hand firmly holds your neck in place

Mockingly courting your desired need for peace

Do it, try to feel anything other than grief

3 hours of rest to let you know you have
a heartbeat, you are still alive

3 hours of rest to let you know in shortness
of breath, the pain of that alive

Lay in your empty room on the hard floor

For anything else merely a deception of
your hidden discomfort inside

Grief with no end, no ease, it just simply is

Neatly tuck it behind your eyes, gloss it
with half-hearted daytime smiles

4am reminds you that you are alone, 4am
reminds you that you wish you weren't

No longer to share a bed with another for they
would know your well-kept secret

Grief shakes you awake in the quiet, every single night

The darkness of an empty room and a hurting
heart, unwanted companions

For the rest of your life

Five

When I was five, I came with no urgency
to be anything except myself

Happiness, sadness, excitement and fear
resided with equal simplicity

There was no awareness of perfect, therefore
there was no pursuit of it

When I was ten, I was told that perfect did exist

There was a map to worth and love, so I hid
my imperfect self and started the chase

When I was fifteen, I battled the urges of holding
on and letting go, no map in hand

I learned to feel shame and to protect myself
with it equally, nothing ever felt perfect

When I was twenty, I knew I was worthless
and I had no hope of finding a map

I felt only sadness and slid in to a hidden existence, invisible

When I was twenty-five, my invisibility hurt, I fought it with anger

I grabbed sadness and carved it in to protective aggression

When I was thirty, I found myself living with my equal

Festering our shame and disdain as two

Misery does love company, but the company
doesn't fill you with love

When I was thirty-five, it crossed my mind
there might be something more

I thought maybe love had just lost its way and my heart forgotten

The last time I had believed in this, a long time ago

When I was forty, I thought back to when I was five

I came with no urgency to be anything except myself

In a matured understanding that I had as a little girl

I remembered I had always been perfect

Love arrived

As when I was five

No Longer

A perfect mixture of magic and reality

Love

A lifetime of tossing glitter in the hope that it gently lands as breath

Leading with, living with, speaking with

Love

The reality is

Surrounded by people who don't believe in magic

Glitter you toss, of no consequence

Unwanted glitter simply collects as apathetic dust on hollow shells

Nothing special, nothing more

The reality is

You will lose your belief in magic

The reality is

I have lost my belief in magic

No longer my inclination

To toss glitter that simply settles as dust

Just Perfect

Beside me

The world settled

The sun rising in the window to my right

The colors dancing off the leaves of the red maple

A snap shot only my eyes will recall

The glass pane open a crack

Allowing a cool summer breeze to kiss my exposed back

The white cotton sheets loosely covering invitation

I look over, there she is

How could a morning be so breathtaking in pure silence?

Sleeping in her perfect self, unaware of my observing love

Absorbing the details of her spine

Starting from the nape of her neck, slowly drawing my eyes down

Running a shortness of breath as I do

The magnificence of her back and shoulders

Details, bends, lines, freckles

She, my original and only painting

The only art my eyes can see

Closing my eyes I take in a deep breath
intoxicating my heart just once more

There she is, just perfect

Observing From the Bottom

Your foot on my head effortlessly holding me under water

Drowned a million times over

Drained of life

Removing my heart from my dead chest for good measure

Spit on my lifeless spirit, watch me sink

Observing you from the bottom

Fully submerged, the water creating a soundless utopia

Clarity in the silence from below

Weightlessness

Somehow, some way

Faith always seems to float my tired shell to the top

Maybe pure hearts have more buoyancy?

While you sleep the tide gently pulls me back to where I belong

Tired, damp

You forget I was born at dawn and always warm again

My heart beats regardless of any flat rhythm, even yours

As I sit on my beach curiosity strikes me

When do they realize?

Good souls never die

They only need rest

My Beautiful Friend

Arms that awkwardly ran in stride with her gazelle like legs

Lips seemingly sized for twice that of her young face

Balanced only by her round plastic rimmed glasses

Her big green eyes magnified for all to see,
tears well up as they teased her

Freckled pale skin that crisped in the summer sun while
her playmates reflected a perfect golden brown

A metal filled mouth forbidding her from
all chewy childhood delights

She was just a little girl who was gifted a shell, a fabric of unique

No better than the pearly straight teeth, flawless skin,
symmetrical features or proportioned length of her peers

Just different

Adults and children alike sputtering her title, the ugly duckling

In my child's eyes she was beautiful, she was my friend

Her big green eyes were full of life that I saw with
more clarity because of those thick round glasses

Her oversized lips would suck up spilled milk off the
kitchen counter twice as fast as mine and we would
giggle with delight slurping our accidental mess

Her long gangly legs made her faster and
dance like none of the other little girls

She was lucky, I admired her

Her freckled sensitive skin meant we got to wear
fancy big hats and sit in the shade and draw
pictures while having picnics and tea parties

She was perfectly beautiful to me

Yet she would quietly cry because she was
always called the ugly duckling

One day she walked out the door and the world took notice

Her long legs and height now that of a model

Once pale freckled skin, flawless from early sensitivity
and care; porcelain like and sought after with envy
by her pimpled and wrinkling mockers

She no longer had a mouth filled with intrusive metal, a million
dollar smile uncovered and used like an assault rifle of charm

Lips that her tiny face had grown in to, beggared
wanting to kiss and photograph with lush delight

The once awkward swing of her body now reflected
in the graceful career of a professional dancer

I sat and watched all those who had damaged
with words, the beautiful little girl

Torn her apart, one insult and exclusion at a time

This day though, they saw her differently

In god like authority now calling her a beautiful swan

They fanned her with flattery, gushing over
how she had come in to her own

As I stood and watched I remembered the
caustic names of not so long ago

Those who had torn her down, now throwing their petals of praise

She was always beautiful to me

Never an ugly duckling and equally insulting
in words, now the beautiful swan

A beautiful little girl grew in to a beautiful woman

Those who made her cry don't deserve to see her incredible smile

She has only ever had one name to me

My beautiful friend

Carved

Standing here

Carved in my own commitment

Did you forget our promise?

Misunderstand our three assaulting words?

Did our "I love you" lack sincerity of depth or
the awareness of a charlatan's truth?

As I stand in my stillness of curiosity, a
suffocating chalky dust settles on me

The moisture from my tears seemingly
seal a stale coating; my new shell

You told me once you should always leave
things better than you found them

I, your thing

Left, swiftly mastered

Better, missed

Standing here carved

Dusting myself off

Black & White

Fault.

I am sorry. I am sorry for not loving you more. I am sorry for not letting you know how many waking moments I thought of you with endless love each day. I am sorry for not taking the time to lie in bed with you every morning just to let you know how much I loved you. I am sorry for not making you feel you were a priority in my life always. I am sorry I did not see the world with you. I am sorry for the times I said things out of hurt or anger when I should have put it aside and told you I loved you. I am sorry for the times you cried because you were unhappy. I did not know and was unable to comfort you. I am sorry that I was not able to fulfill the dreams you thought you would find with me.

Falter.

I thank you. I thank you for laughing with me. I thank you for allowing me to dream. I thank you for making me realize I stood tall beside you, not because of you. I thank you for teaching me that there is as much value in closing a door as there is in opening one sometimes. I thank you for seeing the black in my future so I could be reminded of the light. I thank you for allowing me to open my heart enough to know what it has to offer and the freedom to give it to someone who wants it for eternity. I thank you giving me the opportunity to love myself on a deeper level and live a life more meaningful. I thank you for releasing me to live with truth, integrity and sincerity. I thank you for leaving an opening in my heart and soul for the one who wishes to be there.

Forgive.

I wish. I wish for you to find happiness to the depth of which your heart desires with the stillness and ability to appreciate it for all of its value.

Black and white. Released.

Precious Inamorato

Boxed in the stale attic, her neatly folded love letter

Scripted; precious inamorato

Well-crafted prose, honey drops of poison for unsuspecting ants

Generously dusted promises; confectioners'
sugar over flaked grandiosity

Swells of love so high they couldn't help but float loyalty far away

A forever so long it could never find today

Edges now yellowed, the parchment disintegrating of trust

Decomposing integrity, faint smells of a friendly neighbor's lust

Faded ink telling the tale of a now cancelled play

Squinting for remembrance she drips her remaining
salt hoping for a faint human beat

Sitting alone in the stale attic

Her neatly folded love letter

Precious inamorato

Today

The next day you died

The words drawn in like the underbelly of the tide receding

Invited by gift

The precious rhythm of her heart, delivered in soft powdered ink

Entry through my leather eyes, echoing
deeply in my inner chambers

Words neatly placed beside one another with care

Like clean linen tenderly being hung on
a line to dry in warm sunshine

Merging yesterday with today, beautifully
crashing fragile eloquence

A single floating feather, brushing colors
that paint the existence of life

Today you died

The next day you were born

The Funny Man Next Door

Light your wooden match and toss it on
the alcohol shack you call home

Take your sealed jars of hooch and bury
them deep in your domestic bonfire

Wait for the explosion

Like fireworks on the Fourth of July without the pretty colors

Shards of glass releasing urban stories like an
unexpected assault rifle in the middle of the night

Pay no mind to the children next door watching
the inferno from their windows

Their mother trying to blind their eyes
from the horror that unfolds

The sound of flames collapsing wood, the crunch
of destruction only to be silenced by the screams
of death from the "funny" man next door

They should be dreaming of unicorns and magical
lands tonight, instead they watch the orange burn

Youthful innocence will surely protect them from
the charred roast crisping in the oven

Your love passed out from your disease of choice will
die before she wakes, leaving peaceful hot ash

Her last breath the smoke of your dysfunction

The sirens at your door wake you with agitation only
to be interrupted by the realization you are on fire

You barely stumble out the front door, a dead man walking

The only 12 steps you would ever take

That smell of burning flesh now part of childhood experience

You felt the world looked better through jaundice yellow eyes

Laughing on your porch, your mason jar never out of hand

Until that night you burned it down

Ties

Walking with you across the old abandoned rail bridge

The smell of past life captured in the
warmed stench of creosote ties

Taking careful steps I peep through the
cracks at the unforgiving river below

My anxiously burdened eyes watch as you carelessly walk ahead

My heart uncomfortably paces between feeling and knowing

I question if I envy your bravery or whether
I fear your brazen nature

Only steps from my reach, your foot slips on
a confident tie you once mastered

I watch you free fall in to the raging waters
shifting beneath my comfort

Will your bones be crushed on impact? Will you
effortlessly emerge from the water gliding as you do?

Do I tell you I love you because they will
be the last words you hear?

Or should I have faith in your fall? Is unspoken
trust better than proclaimed attachment?

I lose sight of you in the water, not knowing if you
are swimming below or sinking to the bottom

As I sit in my heartache grieving the unknown

The spirit quietly appears

Not all who fall in to the waters forever disappear

One More Time

You swam out too far

The waves start to roll over your head as the
winds of reality curse their fury

I sit and observe on the safety of my shore

I built it the last time I almost drowned for you

I watch the silent panic in your eyes

Your feet struggling to touch sandy bottom, toes only
feeling sporadic granules to remind you of your danger

Growing weak in your struggle to tread water,
your lungs fill with salty, heavy sadness

Your arms flail as you try to swim toward and swim away

The powerful undercurrent only brings you
back to your place of deathly fatigue

I wave my arms, you cannot see my shore
and you do not see the horizon

Panic and destructive mania as the tide forcefully guides you

Drawing you further in to the ocean where you no longer belong

As I stand on my beach of experience I watch as
you fight for your acceptance and love

Drifting further away in your plea for survival

Losing sight of you under each wave

Do I risk drowning one more time?

Or do I stand on the shore crying as I watch
the storm consume you forever?

Do I drop to my knees and beg that faith finds
you and floats you to stand once more?

Is it ever worth dying to save those who love
the storm more than their shore?

Why Do I know?

Tell me why it is I see the details

Why do I know?

Your favorite delicate flower

Tell me why it is I see the details

Why do I know?

Important days that others let pass by without a thought

Tell me why it is I see the details

Why do I know?

The times I show up without you asking

Tell me why it is I see the details

Why do I know?

Your beautiful scars and the stories they tell

Tell me why it is I see the details

Why do I know?

When you feel the most without a word spoken

Tell me why it is I see the details

Why do I know?

Your inner most struggles

All the details so carefully absorbed

Collected like pieces of extraordinary art

I wonder to myself why it is I see the details and why do I know?

I am in love

A detail you probably should know

Apple Pie

The old mustard colored ceramic bowl
would slide across to the counter

Clanging of stainless steel measuring cups tapping its side

The streamed chaos of electric beaters whirling in my young ears

Furious chops on the old wooden cutting block

My little legs would scurry to the kitchen

With faked curiosity I would chirp; *what are you making?*

Curtly turning in my direction with a concealed smile

Out of my kitchen!

As I laid on the grass dreamily looking at the clouds

The sweet smell of apples baking with the delicate
scent of cinnamon wafting over me

I would poke my cautious eyes through the back door

Pressing laundry, mopping floors, scrubbing pots, the
smell of bleach and starched cleanliness in the air

Quickly looking up only to churn a quick reprimand

Outside!

She never said she loved me

She wasn't one for kisses or hugs

She didn't speak often, never at length

She moved with demanding purpose and solid determination

The sun would start to set over the water

She would sternly call to me once more

Moving faster than my legs could run, grinning ear to ear

Finally

Two neatly cut pieces of pie

She would look over at me with a crooked smile

Eating our pie, sipping our tea

I knew she loved me

So many years later and without fail

The smell of apples baking with that delicate scent of cinnamon

I can never forget how much she loved me with apple pie

Two Poets

One day she exclaimed

I will know she has found *me*

I will inspire *her* swirling verse

One day she exclaimed

I will know I have found *her*

She will inspire *my* swirling verse

One day she exclaimed

No verse will swirl

Having found our wordless love

One day she exclaimed

Two poets fell in love

Labyrinth

Walking quietly beside her, holding her delicate, wise hands

Before me a labyrinth

I stand behind her at its spread of open

She turns to me, tall serenity, layered in seductive enticement

Follow me will you?

Looking deeply in to her eyes

I am washed with equal amounts of indecision

Urge to follow

Urge to lead

Urge to inhale the hushed moment

I know my way through the Labyrinth

Follow me will you?

Her words pull and tug at me like an
invisible rope that is tied to her soul

Tethered to me by my own curiosity of
what moves inside the walls

I follow

She leads, pulls and presses against me with her words
and thoughts as I follow her through the labyrinth

Spin. Glide. Run. Stop. Drift.

Embraced through mazes of wretched
darkness and peaking, frenzied light

Drawn in to complexities I do not know how to navigate

I can't stop the reckless abandon of all that is comfortable

Diving with blind trust in to her pool

I am washed with over whelming love, sadness, fear and fight

Crashing me like waves on to the softness of a white sandy beach

She walks me through her labyrinth of dreamed mazes

My soul entwined through whispered words

Follow me will you

She knows her way

Welcome to her labyrinth

Little Girls Who Met In a Park

The little girls who met in a park

Unruly hair

Freckled noses

Bruised knees

Fawning awkward gaits

Adorning tenuous definitions

Connected by smiles

The little girls who met in a park

Magical dreams carrying hushed thoughts

Hopes of poets, sprinkled with stardust

The strength of warriors standing tall

Unequivocal faith in love not loss

Magnificent spirits

Connected by smiles

The little girls who met in a park

Starting to now silver, walking a confident new pace

Eyes continually mapping an evolving unknown

Stories well read

Unfolding with each new page

Lines now pressing historical marks of laughter and hurt

They arrive tired, forgetting of long ago

With weighted shoulders and complexities

During the pace when they forget who they are

When life seems to have changed

They know where to go and who they will find

Connected by smiles

The little girls who met in a park

Crimson Red

Laying beneath crimson red, reminded of a time before

Thoughts of her rolling

Her violent summer thunder

The collision of dehumanized pressure

Soaring temperature, polarized

Snapping

Cracking

A recollection of ceremoniousness love, insulating its unpredictable expansion

Memories of lying beneath the crimson red, one irrevocable summer

The fury of her abrupt storm

Violent

Snapping

Cracking

The colossal timber vituperated

No longer etched in time

Laying beneath crimson red

The sorrowful destruction of her conclusive futile storm

My Window

Laying on the cool cotton, a window that I have
looked out a thousand times before

My heart rapidly transposes time through this singular view

Seasons that have passed, souls not forgotten

Leaves that have fallen among seeds that were quietly rooting

Blossoms that came, whispering renewal

The transformation of the walls surrounding the frame

Reflecting love that once was

Pictures

Forever etched in the deep canyons of my heart

Snap shots of the awakening of dawn

A thousand times before I have looked out my window

A thousand times before

It was beautiful

Forever Closed

I looked out the same window

Eyes filled with fresh tears of old loss

This time

The birds seemingly gone, no longer singing their songs

The red maple that once blew whispers of hope

Its leaves now dry and sorrowfully still

The billowy clouds that transported states of magical gaze

Replaced with muted grey, lacking in description of kind

A sacred spot where I slept with my dreams

Now nothing more than a functional bed, lacking comfort or rest

Layering of time and cherished thoughts
held such a magical space

Seemed to float away, nothing more than
common dust in summer rays

Grief without dreams, grief without hopes, grief without beliefs

I closed my eyes and my once poetic
window now frames a dull reality

No leap of faith, glimmer of hope or wink of magic

I opened my eyes, I wonder

Are they forever closed?

All This

I wish I was…

A painter

Brushing in color my adoration for only you

Such a beautiful sight it stands in a gallery of one

A writer

Scripting love stories to settle the dustiest corners of your fears

Pressed with scented flowers between each page,
as a reminder of your beautiful soul

A preacher

Speaking the gospel of hope and love with trusted conviction

Igniting the faith of your heart back in to your cautious bones

A book

Questions you carry about love, you would
simply open it and find your answers

Reading yes, mine is true

A blanket

Providing you quiet warmth without condition or request

Always there, always faithful

If your heart would allow

If you could just look up

If you could see my eyes

In the silence, there it would be

All this

For you

Inside of me

The Only Objects

There comes a time when you question
human spirit, your belief in love

The prick of a new thorn reminding you of the last

Infection almost won that time

Scarred and damp, you were left on a shore without compass

The stale smell, reminiscent of that time you started to rot

Tightly pinch your eyes shut

Sew them closed with apathetic thread

Hold your heart, deeply cage it inside sharp walls

Do not let the spectators at the zoo see it

Definitely don't let them feel it

Do not

Feed the animals

Maybe the past won't see you if you don't make eye contact

Present might not notice and keep walking

Perhaps future will remain in perfect wax form

Melting only if you get too close to sun

Stay safe

Stay cold

Memory has a tricky way of finding you

Life, a funny way of tapping your conscience awake

Even if only in your dreams

Sitting in lotus, looking for objects of reality

I hear my breathing

I feel my heart

The only objects of reality remaining

My human spirit

My belief in love

Foolish Human

Foolish human

To think there is a sensibility to love is
to assume you control the tide

The ocean does not argue with the moon

Cognitive negotiations do not occur to decide the
rise and fall of something greater than us

No manual is consulted on how to shift the
waves or dim the evening light

Sensibility may try to whisper that love is wasted, futile, a mistake

The king tide happens when the Earth, Moon and
Sun are aligned at perigee and perihelion

Like true love; uncommon, intense and powerful

You can toss bitter words towards the Earth, Moon and Sun

Curse them for their non-conformity and disruptive ways

But true love and the king tide are not made by human sensibility

Foolish human

If you must

Lock yourself inside at night and stay clear of the ocean

I should warn you though, the king tide continues

As does true love

Now

As the winter air bit at her cheeks in her forest of thoughts

Her heart weighted, indulging in sadness

A past heavy in disappointment

Her future never arriving between blinks

She gave herself permission

You may now

Close the gap of your expectations

Family looks as it feels

Not what is written in fiction

Home is not made of carefully placed
cushions or well-appointed rugs

She was not "them," "she" or "her"

She was "I"

"I" knew happiness was to be felt, not chased

"I" felt love for people, not things

"I" knew time was wealth, not income

"I" gave permission

To let "them" be the holder of expectations

"I" will live a beautiful life

Love Should

If it is real, does it find its way home?

Or stay forever lost in broken past?

If it beats once, will it twice?

Or simply bestow us with snapshots to remember flickering nights

Are reminders there to grate our chamber back to life?

Rattle our ribs

Tap and pang

Force uncontrolled crimson flow

If it drifts away so effortlessly

Are we intuitively beckoned to warm the next
lonely drifter beseeching our shore?

If our vessel was split in disrepair

Do we sink more gracefully by drilling further holes?

Is apathetic posture the cognitive kinship to maintaining float?

Or does its weight fill our spaces while emptying our bowls?

Darkness doesn't give a shadow, it stands alone

Only light appreciates and invites the company of mirror

If heart ache is real, then love once was

If heart ache should never happen

Then I guess

Love always should

Rest

When it all draws in too close

Lay your head on my lap

Dehydrated chambers will beat again like new birth

Welcome the apathy of your dreams with
relaxed eyes and tender hands

Weightlessly floating on foundation of secure promise

A precious heart surrounds itself by
continual bloom of respect and trust

Gentle nature blows away accumulated dust

Loyalty suspending particulates of once weighted
thought to dance in summer rays

When it all draws too close

Lay your head on my lap

Rest in my love

What If We Are Home?

What if we are home?

Maybe the bed we are to make, is one another

Pictures to hang on blank walls, forged only by us

When did we tuck our paint brushes of
creation away in fear of hurt?

Were colors meant to dry up in the warmth
of the safety of a lonely existence?

To be admired from afar in cracked pots of weathered silence?

Words of love and loss musing to be the only
entry to the doorway of destiny

Or just an echo of a distant past with lingering bad taste

What if we are home?

The Run

A thoroughbred race horse about to break
their leg before the finish line

Running

Adrenaline injected thoughts, anticipated marrow snapping

Put your heavy values down and wait for the crunch

Shhh...do you hear the echo of a heart locked
in uncomfortable burst among trees?

Chased by possibility and stillness, moving forward for what?

Run away or towards

Maybe stand still and wait, do nothing

Why am I lost on the trail again?

Ask the little girl, she seems to know how to find her way around

I wonder if I can find her with the noise of heavy
rusted chains, scented with vinegar past

Branches breaking under feet

Reminders of the first time running the trail

Running away from dead

Holding life by her precious hand upon exit

A dog named karma always seems to meet
me somewhere along the path

A reminder

I don't run and karma is just a dog

I was lost in the trails again today

The little girl found me as I was chasing my
spirit and running away from fear

She smiled and reminded me

I have never been lost

I was just finding my path

Trash

Dusting off shelves

Clearing the clutter

Polishing pictures with your rancid butter

Boxing up old

Mourning no loss as I clean through tears

Loving you too long spoke to all my fears

Ridding of you, discarding our past

Committing now to solitary chaste

Your abusive nature

The only thing true

Chew on that

My memory of you

Cleansing my soul

Bleaching my eyes from heinous sight

My white flag on fire, no longer a fight

A charlatan

Selling nothing but lies

Your dead heart swarming with brainless flies

Mopping away your dirty ash

Blowing it off

Human trash

You ruined the white linen

Painting the walls with black tar

In place of my heart

A buried scar

I have sat in discomfort

Drowning in your evil stay

Watching my life slowly slip away

After years of ingesting your acidic piss

I learned to stand up and say

Not this

As I clean up your mess of narcissistic gore

You are no longer welcome

Not any more

The Fox

The sharp teeth of little red fox holding down
rabbit by his tender, fragile neck

Tell me rabbit before I take my last glorious bite

Do you fear your untimely, pending death?

Not at all dear fox, my fear is something so much more

Life as it currently exists, as you have me
helplessly pinned to the floor

Comparatively death is just an end and sadness I will not feel

You my friend can celebrate a lovely rabbit meal

Then answer me this

Brave little rabbit

Does my darkness make you tremble in your tiny soul?

Oh, not at all little fox

I embarrassingly tend to fall easy prey

My light is bright, my heart whole

I naively dance to poetic romantic cajole

Most likely this makes me somewhat of a hunters bore

Perhaps though

My love will make me taste of sweetness that much more?

Dear fox

I humbly ask you this before you take your final bite

Does my pure love, taking it away

Not give you any sort of fright?

Of course not foolish rabbit

I devour as I choose

My furry meal you make no difference

You rabbits will always lose

Then dear fox

I will rest easy in death with the wisdom I have shared

As you take me away

My heart is full, knowing I have always truly cared

Trusting you know you will be taking my
life with assured understanding

Love truly is wonderful

A precious and special light

It is only my loss

That will keep you up at night

Flowing

Was the desire for love and family so blind to reality?

Simply childish day dreams deeply rooted in innocence

Did we strengthen our glittery threads of
forever with a delusional belief of hope?

Prematurely running towards something our
youthful nature did not fully yet recognize?

Was it the plan to carve our hearts with bitter loss and betrayal?

To forever close the magic show, our circus of happy

Walling it off with a rigid cognitive existence

Maybe…

Ego needed to be told

Ego needed to learn that our life purpose is not to chase and attain

Ego needed to learn we are meant to be quiet
and feel as we find one another

Ego knew too much and nothing at all

Ego rode the first pretty horse that pranced by posing as a unicorn

Perhaps our lesson of impatience was part of a plan

A step towards the knowing wink of arriving love

Earlier desires running our river dry, curiously
tapping us on destiny's shoulder

Reminding us of the sounds of water coming back

Maybe to fill it once again we just need to
believe, the river never stopped flowing

Dearest Muse

Dearest Muse,

I poetically and apologetically must let you go

I will try to explain as I let myself flow

You; unforgettably with a desired spark in your eye

Me; watched seductively as you sipped on your rye

Your skin as supple as a Georgia peach

Laying quietly beside me on our romantic beach

Write me a poem, make it all about me

Please, pretty please, forever we will be

Your words left me hanging with utter delight

My eyes seeing only your dreamy wish for me to write

Over taken by your glorious narcissistic being

You my muse felt incredibly freeing

Hurriedly writing words of deep observation

You; fanning my ridiculous furious concentration

With great trepidation of a vulnerable poet

I shared my words and wouldn't you know it

As I exposed my love and my deep inner workings

You responded with *crickets chirping*

Sorry my muse who was once so incredibly desired

You my love are poetically fired

Watching You Burn

I find it curious the anger you so tenderly feed, mother bird
mouthing food to her young dependent. Let me light a fire to keep
you warm. Trust me as I pour gasoline on it and let you burn.

I find it curious how your hate sets forth to devour. Do
you think your brush burning protects your house?
Does the fire you set somehow control the hour?

I find it curious. When the fire dies will you stop the
burning? Or does the anger stay and continue on?

I find it curious why you feel the need.

To set your fires and watch it all burn.

Drifting

Her shell weighted and dry, mite like irritation upon touch

Wearing her enthusiasm like stained, tattered lace

Squinted sophistication beneath an inferior history

Grotesquely adorned with rusted shackles that hold no key

Eyes drawn with the burden of memory

Flickering affect

A gentle hand passing words, supposition of light

Reminded of painted memories of when she once closed her eyes

For a moment her onerous cloak of thoughts drift

A lightness of breath

In the distance she sees it

Happiness

My Thing

They told me I should go to yoga, it will make me feel happy. As I posed in downward dog, the man in front of me farted. Nobody laughed. I thought to myself it was much more fun when I was a child. Me and my brother would cup farts in our hands and shove them in each other's faces and then laugh hysterically. I thought if someone farting in my face is supposed to make me happy, surely we should be laughing. Maybe yoga isn't my thing.

They told me I should take a spin class, I will feel invigorated. I liked the music but sitting on that hard uncomfortable seat for an hour made my vagina hurt. I thought back to other times that my vagina hurt. They were much more fun than spin class. I thought if my vagina is going to hurt surely a bike seat is not the optimum cause. Maybe spin class isn't my thing.

They told me I should drink smoothies from the trendy new juice bar, it will make me healthy. For twelve dollars I ordered a strawberry, banana, wheat grass, chia seed, hemp powder, extra protein power bomb. The people all around me looked very healthy and it tasted just fine. As I sat there though, I reflected on drinking strawberry, banana margaritas with my friends. Somehow I thought, wouldn't it be more healthy and fun to have smoothies with tequila and a side of laughter? Maybe drinking smoothies isn't my thing.

I didn't know what to do, no option seemed to fit or make any sense. So I sat in the park by myself and fed the ducks. The ducks didn't seem to mind if I farted. They weren't so bothered that my vagina hurt or that I was drinking a margarita from a thermos. I suddenly felt happy, invigorated and healthy.

Ducks in the park, they are my thing.

Bazooka

We were out on a first date when she asked me to empty my purse. She confidently told me that you can tell everything about a person by its contents. Let me see it she said curtly. I obliged.

Tumbling out came a wallet, a pen, a cheque book, an individually wrapped piece of Bazooka gum, and a Swiss army knife. Looking dreadfully disappointed she said to me, you must be a very boring person.

I smiled in reply. *I am sorry I just realized I must leave.* Looking offended she asked why.

You see, I am reminded that I stabbed someone in the neck with my pen earlier and used my Swiss army knife to dismember their body. I left them on my kitchen counter and it is probably going to start to smell if I don't move it to my freezer soon. You know, it was just one of those arguments where they wanted cash, while I wanted to write a cheque.

Looking horrified and confused she watched as I unwrapped my piece of Bazooka gum and popped it in my mouth. I gnawed away on that big, hard piece of obnoxious pink gum like a 4 year old. I placed the little comic that was wrapped inside in front of her. Whilst slobbering pink bubble gum in undisguised delight I said you should read it. They are really very funny, oh by the way I only chew Bazooka gum because of the comic inside.

I guess she was right, the contents of your purse do say everything about you.

I am a funny woman.

The Canary

You probably should not mention how much you love her

Don't tell her you think it might last a lifetime

Or it may flow in to the next

Too much, too much

I think best to discuss it over tea, something
fruity and slighted with spice

Her palate is particular, make note

Not too hot, not too cool

Interesting porcelain tea cups only

They should oddly belong together but not match

She will need something to look at as you speak

Most likely she will twiddle her fingers like tangled yarn

Put some sweets on a well-appointed plate to distract her

You know, about the whole love thing

Best not to bring up love more than once, she is fickle that way

The movies and love songs tell you to exclaim
your love loudly and with the roar of lion

The thing is though she is better than the movies and love songs

She is the gentle sound of the silver birch
leaves that rustle in the wind

She is the moonlight that peeps through the cracks
of the window in the middle of the night

She is the sensitivities that only the canary notices

Speak quietly, find your nervous voice that you don't like to use

The one that only your heart knows

Promise her only one thing, that you will
hold her hand for a lifetime

For the canary knows

A fleeting heart is worth far less

Than the one who with sincerity, simply wants
to hold her hand for the rest of her life

Bowing at the Threshold

Gracefully bowing at the threshold

Emptying her mind of worries

Heart filling with joy

This moment

Now

A quiet reminder of the many she almost lost

One hundred and eight rhythmic reverberations, transcending

Each breath gently blowing away clouds of uncertainty

Opening his eyes, he stares, drained of what little life he ever had

I am dying

She smiles in long pause, can I tell you a secret?

We all are

My Wooden Pew

Looking through the stained glass window

Such encapsulating colors deliver painted sunshine

Little dust particulates floating in air like messages from angels

Lost in the patina of my wooden pew

I wonder how many others have sat here days before me

Who did they drop their salted tears for?

You

Boxed in front of me

Sleeping so peacefully

Yet I don't see you there

Your day of shrine, murmuring verse
from someone you didn't know

I wonder if you hear us

Do you see who has come to worship?

Is that your hand I feel on my heart?

Or do I write intellectual stories to quell my own sadness

I see you everywhere, feel your touch

Looking through the stained glass window

Let Us

Let us fall in love

Not in the common form

Ink your thoughts just for me

I will wait for them to arrive in the post

Hearing only your voice as I read them

Slow drawn romance

One excited smile at a time

We will make it special

Let's send dozens of letters

Waiting painfully long days for their arrival

I want to fall in love with your mind, you with mine

I want to dream of the day we can finally touch

Let's believe that our hearts are important and love rare

Building longevity one hand written thought at a time

Let's not meet for months, only travelling far to do so

We will stop time to be in our own

Let us fall in love

Not in the common form

The Moment Heaven Called You

It comes with no end

A progressive continuum of missing you

I see you in moments of laughter

I hear you in the lonely silence

I feel you holding my arm when you are with me

If I could just have one more day

Another dinner filled with the sound of your laughter

To sit and watch you from across the table

One more hug

One more I love you

One more moment

My mind tries to reason that you are gone
but my heart will not listen

You are in the stars

You are in the tranquility of the ripples on the water

Your angelic kisses left in serendipitous gifts

Every beautiful moment, you are seen

I did not know grief

I did not know how deeply I loved

I did not know how hard it would be

I did not know how precious it all was

Until the moment heaven called you

When She Goes Silent

When she goes silent, you need to listen

Find her in the dusted corner

Blinds drawn

A room for one

Black and white with broken wings

Her words her mind, unspoken her heart

Darkness, struggle and ferocity will shake you in prose

Inner depths echo only in her eyes

Silent

She screams to be heard, never held

Find her heart and warm it carefully

When she goes silent

You need to listen

At the Foot of the Camellia Tree

She weeps at the foot of the Camellia tree

Long standing in years, an epicenter of memories

Rooted legacy, family

Seventy years of love, death, survival, breaking
points, bottoms and glorious resurrection

Captured in thoughts, memories, dreams,
photos, poems, mind and heart

The Camellia tree, part of our blood

Beginning, middle and end

The story it holds, life

Her life, their life, our life

From an outsider's eye, it is just a tree

To those who have stood at its foot, more

A legacy rich in our hearts

Her parents teaching, eventually legacy is all that remains

Spoken to her with love at the foot of the Camellia tree

As children she whispered to us the same secret

We must keep living our story, it is our legacy to one another

We are family

The Camellia tree, soon no longer to stand

Our rich understanding of growth, family and legacy

The reason we are rebuilding our place of worship

It is our turn now to build and carry hundreds of
years that have passed by planting new seeds

The legacy of the roots that were planted
at the foot of the Camellia tree

Our young children watching and learning,
it is our turn to whisper

She weeps at the foot of the Camellia tree

For it was never just a tree, it is the passing of generations

A marking of her own extensions and limits in time

Forever more it will live in our hearts

The legacy, the roots and the story of the Camellia tree

Stiletto

Your words

Drip with extravagance, *Stuart Weitzman* stilettos

Silky smooth elegance, money on wheels

Still, just stilettos

Do some words have higher value?

Do the mouths that pour them have increased credibility?

Or is value something else?

Does loftier expression help us walk better?

Do we speak more eloquently with diamonds on our toes?

Are we to be revered and trusted because
our feet are bound by intellect?

Is love more meaningful when it is poetic?

Does sincerity live in 3 tiny words or one action?

I love you, silence

Your words make me wonder

Are they worth the price or simply just another pair of stilettos?

Neatly

You, throwing your wet blanket of darkness on her warm fire

No care, no regard

The purpose?

You fear her happiness, you swarm goodness
because you have lost your own

Swinging your verbal machete while blindfolded

Dripping in the blood of her spirit, relishing in her destruction

Mindless amputation, dimming her light to lighten your dark

No reprieve until you are both drenched in maimed destitution

One ravished and emotionally bleeding, her

Dead eyes pointing out useless fragility, you

Dear human, she is not darkness, she is IN darkness

Mistake not the two

She will stand up, not speak and not fight

My light will flicker to remind her of her own

Put on your sunglasses as it will burn as I
walk her out of your dark abyss

Tucking you in neatly with care under your wet blanket

It will be

Just you

Kicks

Victims and Villains

Episodic love and hate

Who wore it best?

Who remains more neatly pressed

Splattered egos

Dysfunctional folklore

Find your role, eat or be eaten

Ultimate devour

Emotionless lovers

Not my kicks

708 Days

708 days later

Sitting in the same quiet spot

The sun still warming her cheeks

Pressed with lines of days passed

The trees have grown taller

Roots stronger

A quiet wisdom carried in leaves, whispers in the breeze

The same storm arrived once more

The same storm that ravished 708 days earlier

She, the storm leaving trees fallen

She, the storm that left roots unearthed and vulnerable

She, the storm whipping delicate leaves about carelessly

The same storm arrived 708 days later

This time

Her tree taller, stronger

Her roots stayed

Her leaves beautifully speaking calm clarity

Now, when she, the storm, arrived 708 days later

The tree spoke

Not this time

Tuesday Nights

Knocked over without regard like Tuesday night bowling pins

Cheap stale beer coating his stained
yellow teeth, toxic abusive spite

The player; never a passing thought as
to the destruction of the pins

Celebrating her only in the affection of his deplorable sins

Bracing herself deeply in emotionless red clay

Conceiving the strike will hurt less if her movement is taken away

Now buried in survival up to her neck

The player keeps playing

The pins knocked down, committed unscheduled hate

Served with dysfunctional glee on his domestic plate

The pin one day tired of being his game

Growing legs, she limps down his dark alley of unrelenting play

Brushing off her layers

Giving it one quick, last blow

Dusting her history, the neighbors would never know

Looking coldly at the bowler's dark dead eyes

She picks up his balls, calmly walking away

The game finally over

In one simple play

One day

I am sorry

My light flows against your undercurrents of rage

My kind words feather your inferno of darkness

My vulnerability threatens your inner loathing

My eyes see past your charcoal haze

My heart dismisses your abomination for purity

My soul is walled off from your bludgeoning effect

I am sorry

To stand on my foundation

To observe with love, your personal destruction

To watch you recklessly dive in to your empty pool

To witness the journey of your deepening bottom

To lay my head down in the safety of respected love

To not interrupt the harsh polarity of our paths

I am sorry

For the ferocity in which you will fall

For the unimaginable depth of pain you will feel

For the nights you will cry alone with echoes screaming your past

For silence in your excruciating emotional detox

For the itch that you will not know how to appease

For loneliness that will murmur tales of worthlessness

For the days that will bleed in to one another,
with only the drone of despair

One day

One day you will have a glimmer of light

One day you will feel the warmth of kindness

One day you will smell the sweetness of vulnerability

One day you will reach out to the curious nature of purity

One day you will remember a beautiful soul

It is only then

One day

You will know why

I am sorry

Dusted Souls

Dusted souls

Eyes embraced in a hushed understanding

Considerate words of kindness exchanged

Demonstrating a truth of existence

Beneath the confines of social graces

Erupting preoccupations for undisputed spirit

A dusted soul as one

Observing as one

Writing as one

Sitting on her bench of one

The dust starts to collect on her frame

As she blows off gathering apathy

Another sits on her bench

Observing as one

Writing as one

Eyes embraced in a hushed understanding

Two

Dusted souls

In the Corner of Her Sky

In the corner of her sky

The grey began to roll in, uncompromising

The darkness ridged, uncomfortably
drenching her like many times before

With sharp panic she purposefully dances
to avoid its debilitating nature

Moving with just enough precision to keep an eye on the beast

Covering her ears of its sorrowful tales filled with empty sins

With lashing words and an unforgiving memory

She stopped

Standing

Scared

Bravely she looks her beast in the eye

In quiet

In silence

It no longer envelopes her as it once had

Her heart knows her beast only resides

In the corner of her sky

Her Heart

It rolled over her like the morning fog

Raw and still, she breathlessly watched as it devoured

Absorbed through each pore; the water heavy
and weighted, suffocating her spirit

Damp and paralyzed

Faint and muffled, a deeply buried beat,
unknowingly keeping her warm inside

Quietly reminding her of love

With a dull gasp, the fog recedes to devour another shore

There she sits on her beach, ravaged and vulnerable

Her heart, her awakened companion

Perfect stillness

Warmth begins to fill her, burning away
the quiet memory of the fog

Watching the waves, she realizes

She is home

Her heart

When I Was a Little Girl

When I was a little girl, the cherry blossoms would
fall from the tree, it was my pink spring snow

When I was a little girl, I would skip when
walking was too mundane

When I was a little girl, I would welcome the cold rain
droplets to kiss my face and nourish my soul

When I was a little girl, I would look under rocks at
the beach, watching the tiny crabs scurry away

When I was a little girl, I would lay on the grass in warm
sun and dreamily look at the clouds as they passed

When I was a little girl, I laughed with my
friends until my cheeks hurt

When I was a little girl, I knew that I could
be anything I wanted to be

When I was a little girl, being kind and good was
always more important than being right

When I was a little girl, I knew what love was
and how it felt with great confidence

When I grew up

I learned that everything I ever needed to know in life

I already knew

When I was a little girl

Her bed

Laying in her bed

Rising from her lioness slumber

She stretches her long body with a relaxed caution

Sounds of today dancing through the window

Delicate scent of a fresh spring morning

Penetrating her soul, deeply inhaling a new day

Song birds reminding her of opportunity and innocence

Yesterday washed away

Quiet in her heart

Crisp white cotton sheets adorn her perfectly reckless body

Speaking no words she looks over to me

Behind her thoughtful gaze

A lifetime of stories that wrap around me with curiosity

Sitting with locked eyes

No space between us

I sit in this moment, as it rushes through my being

I look in her eyes and know my heart has spoken

Laying in her bed

Copper

The gun shots fire, no longer offering sharp echoes in my soul

My spark floated away with your loosely promised words

Eyes that entranced me, merely blinks clocking empty seconds

Wrapped in your pretty shell, smile for the camera

Your hair looks great, don't worry no one
will notice your insincerity

Delivering romance again on your hammered copper platter

Forgive me as I yawn

My tears aren't available to turn the copper green this time

Canyons ran deep with hopes of weave, tangle, press and twist

Barren spaces, clay and dust

Miles of nothing, as far as my eye for you can see

Do you hear that?

It is the echo of the space you once occupied, and

The sound of, I no longer care

Tangled Fond

Our eyes catch one another

Naturally drawn as when our gaze once
shared the intimacy of a bed

Like a silent pull dividing a crowd to find our meet

Flashes of locked eyes pour over me with candlelight
that flickered across our skin that one night

Now a discarded ball of wax that sits
beside an empty bottle of merlot

The ceiling fan that turned in wobble periodically
breezing over our bare backs

Now turned off as the cool fall has arrived

We greet on the street with courteous hellos

Gracious, polite, thick with unspoken

Such fondness that history entwined us in limb and vine

In fondness lays the beautiful eloquence of our poem

With our poems end lays the reality that we never wrote a story

For, fondness feather fans deep sincerity of our moments

While love continues to catch our eyes

Writing beyond tangle and a story that never ends

Lard

I met a woman who made her living charming the pure

Slipping the wedding band off the hand of
the bride still warm in her death

A hundred-dollar bill wiping the tears of
the groom ripe from his pocket

The first to hold in comfort with sociopathic embrace,
she brazenly spoke of her slippery way

Glorious in ease and nature's path, flash
a smile, glitter it with a wink

Reap away, write only of her in the darkest ink

Exclaiming the banana peel on the ground is
never to blame for unfortunate slip

Place your hate in those who litter unwanted waste,
doubly slap your ignorance for trusting any step

You see it is only you who is to blame, she belched her way
through life drenching herself in the spoiling lard of attainment

A rosary hung from her rear view mirror offering religious
beliefs like a prostitute who advertises safe sex

I asked with curiosity, when your lights start to
dim do you think your soul will still travel

Scoffing at my naivety and trusting ways she
crossed my street wishing me good day

Reminding me, if you see her coming always walk the other way

Type A

I give you thanks for the bitter you poured in my morning
coffee, I used it to aid in the digestion of your aging sour milk

The blood you drew in your paper cut war "love letters lost"

Make me suffer, my unburdened heart allows for
immediate burn and the intended sting

The good news, I know how to feel and I still hear the birds sing

Unfamiliar with how to eloquently die I dripped
blood type A in to my hereditary ink

I used the blood you so wished would drain me of life

To write my poems of love and happiness
during my sleepless nights

We all makes our choices, our stories we tell

Only some of us have learned the power of a deepening well

Set me on fire, cut me with your heinous disregard

Try to stomp me to death with the insanity of your being

I learn with each kick, the day I left you would always be freeing

I will simply turn your hate in to words written in red

As you will see

It was me who was cut but only you who has bled

We Need Only

Our eloquent dance

Finger and limb weave quietly, perfect
poetic fit in the safety of our wrap

Our shared breathing, short of ordinary

Feel the surge, ride, flow and fight

Cautious vulnerability slowing our tangle of know,
anticipated extraordinary trapped in reminded glow

Proclamation wanting to release with roar, feel the wet
warmth of August thunder knowing you want more

Her presence carries familiar timelessness, so curious

Connection that runs well below the blink of this
life, make and devour balanced in equal bite

Pulse and heart that comfortably itch placing
us exactly where we belong

If we dare

We need not discuss or consult an instruction book

We need not set the clock on perfect cognitive time

We need only to meet for common embrace, not based on chance

Welcome to our life my dear, may I have this dance?

Acknowledgments

Lori Popadiuk at www.loripop.com for your continual inspiration, laughter and support.

Isabelle Swiderski at www.seven25.com for your incredible talent creating this beautiful cover and your precious friendship.

Photographer, Wendy D at www.wendyd.ca for the magnificent photo that wraps the cover of Dusted Words.

To my Mom, for continuing to recite poetry to me for as long as I can remember (even when I sighed and rolled my eyes). I didn't know it at the time but it was going to be one of the greatest gifts my heart would ever know.

To my children, Kate and Noah. I breathe goodness because you both live in my heart. Words will never capture how deeply I love you. The world is magnificent because you are in it.

For the women who gave these poems breath. Thank you for sharing your hearts and stories with me.

www.ingramcontent.com/pod-product-compliance
Lightning Source LLC
Chambersburg PA
CBHW051841040426
42447CB00006B/639